Why I Walk with His Majesty

Lady Jammie Desiree

To order additional copies of this book, contact:
Xlibris
1-888-795-4274
www.Xlibris.com
Orders@Xlibris.com

ISBN:	Softcover	978-1-7960-8596-9
	Hardcover	978-1-7960-8597-6
	EBook	978-1-7960-8595-2

Library of Congress Control Number: 2020902075

Print information available on the last page

Rev. date: 02/07/2020

(Introduction) By: Lady Jammie Desiree.

Konjo Blessings and love and Honour. To all my family and friends and to the world of books & readers. I pray with the writing of this short story. I have answered, many questions. You have ask of me, of his Majesty. Emperor Haile Selassie the first.

Many have asked me,why do you believe that the Emperor Haile Selassie the first. Is the Conquering lion of the Tribe of judah?.

Well now you can read, study research his Majesty Emperor Haile Selassie the first. By reading my story, of why I walk with him, in his teachings. And why the people of Rastafari, love and adore him, too.
Hallelujah. Glory hallelujah.

Remember this is my own testimony
And Spiritual intervention, and experiences
Of my personal growth and understanding of the teachings and principles and, words of power, of His Majesty. Emperor Haile Selassie the first. And my love of the
Holy Messiah. Jesus Christ. Lord & Savior.

Table of Contents

The Spirit of the Redeemer

Haile Selassie the first. Was crowned Prince.
Of The Ethiopian. Empire . From 1916 to 1928. And then he later became king .

From 1928-1930. And then Emperor.
From 1930-1974. Born under The Same sign as, I a Leo. Born July 23, 1892.
In Ejersa Goro. Ethiopia.

His full name is : Ras Tafari Mckeonnen.
He was assassinated . August 27, 1978.
In Addis Ababa, Ethiopia.

Emperor Haile Selassie the first. Was 83 years of age, during his murdering . He died at The
jubilee Palace. His death was ruled out as a death by strangulation.

Even though, his death was ruled out as a strangulation. We know that the government, still
may want to reopen the case. And investigate the true cause
Of death and why? He was murdered.
And by who.

Crown prince of Ethiopia

Haile Selassie the first. Was crowned
Prince of Ethiopia. A Empire.
His Coronation was
November 2, 1930. King of ok Kings. Of Ethiopia. JAH Rastafari.

Conquering lion of the Tribe of judah. Elect of God. Chief Commander. Order of the Star of
Ethiopia. He Was Establish as a order. Of knighthood.

The badge of The Order

The badge of order. Of Emperor Haile Selassie the first. JAH Rastafari.

The order was given and established.
To honor foreign, and, domestic civilian and military .

Honorary knighthood. Order of the Grand cross.

The order of St. Michael and, St. George.

Power of The Trinity

Haile Selassie. Internationalist views, led to
Ethiopia becoming a charter member of The
United Nations. At The league of Nations.

Emperor Haile Selassie the first.
Has been criticized by some, historians. For being rebellious among his piers, of that time.

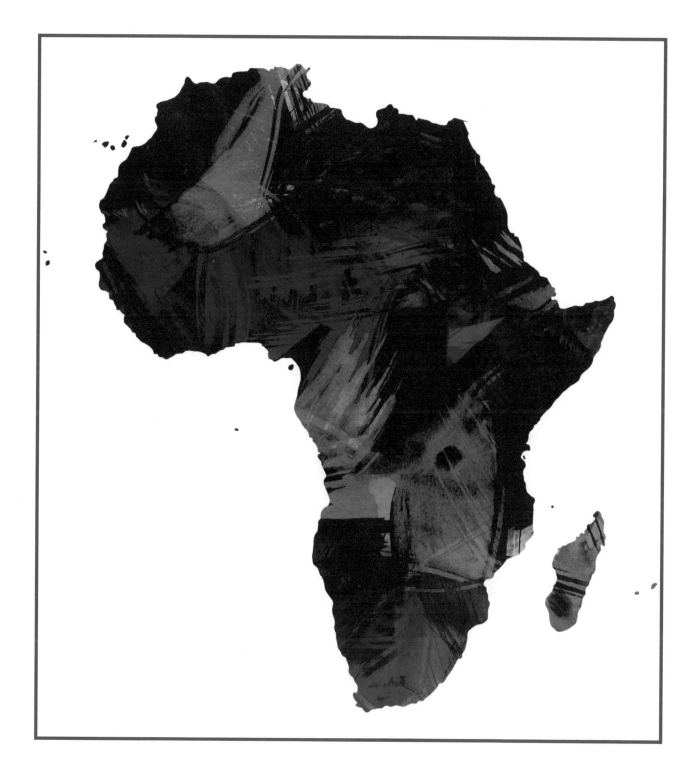

In his 58 years of leadership. In Ethiopia.
First as Regent, then Emperor. Haile Selassie of Ethiopia. Accumulated many
Honorary medals. Both domestically and Abroad.

As a result of his Numerous visits to foreign lands. He was considered one of the most
decorated personas . In Human history.

In 1909 . Emperor Haile Selassie the first.
Was rewarded . The Star of Ethiopia.
This was establish, as a. Order of Knighthood. Of the Ethiopian Empire.
Founded, by the Negus Of Shoa.
And later. Emperor of Ethiopia.

Solomonic Dynasty

(House of Solomon)

Emperor Menelik

The Solomonic Dynasty. (Solomonic Restoration). The historical Solomonic Dynasty. Started in the Dynasty of
1270- 1636 B.C.

Emperor Yekuno Amlak . Became Emperor. And he declared, to be the lineal descent of menelik the 1st. Son of King Solomon.
And Queen Sheba. He ended his Short Rule
Of Ethiopia in the Solomonic Dynasty.

The Solomonic Dynasty also known as the House of Solomon. Is the former, ruling. Of the Ethiopian Empire. The Dynasty members
Claim lineal descent from the biblical. King Solomon. And the Queen Sheba.

The Solomonic Dynasty

The Solomonic Dynasty consist of the following.

1. Front house -House of David.
2. Current head. - zera yacob Amha Selassie
3. Final Ruler- Emperor Haile Selassie the first.
4. Place of Origin. : Horn Of Africa.
5. Founded: 900 B.C.

According to the kebra Negast. (Glory of The)Kings)

Queen Makeda (The Queen of Sheba)
And (King Solomon) had a child together.
And his name was Menelik. Originally name
Ebna la -hakim. (son of the wise)
He was the first Solomonic Emperor of Ethiopia. From The Tribe of judah.

The connection between (Israel and, Ethiopia) doesn't end in Africa . But the Solomonic Dynasty extends, all the way to The Caribbean people of the world. The Solomonic Dynasty that was here on the earth. In the days of King Solomon, Queen Sheba. Are still here, in this time. If we look at the slave trade. From Africa to the Americas and to the Caribbean. We can see
The ancestory is in our people of the Caribbean.

We see this resemblance in the everlasting truth and power of the teachings of his Majesty. Emperor Haile Selassie the first.
The message among the people of the Caribbean. Is loud, & clear. The love the Jamaican culture share, with the covenant of king David, and the covenant of king Solomon. And the covenant of Queen Sheba.

We see this practice among our people of Rastafari. On a continuing basis. We see the teachings of Rastafarianism. That has now spread by sound, word, power.. through the music of the Caribbean world of Reggae. We see these teachings of his Majesty.
Through the dreadlock hair styles.

We see this teaching of His Majesty Emperor Haile Selassie the first. Through the livity of the world of Rastafari. More & more generations of world, are following this teaching. Holy Allah jah Rastafari. This is the blessings of judah. That has manifested, amplified through the internet and music, propaganda, language, arts, culture.

The Teachings of his Majesty. Is that which identifies with the covenant of king Solomon and the congregation of Queen Sheba.

From Israel to The Caribbean islands

The Slave Trade routes, that lead our people
To the Caribbean island.
From Ethiopia to Caribbean. The slave trade
Ran from the east, to the west.

The Caribbean island is made up of
Cuba, Jamaica, and Haiti Santo domingos, PuertoRico .. These are the children who were traded from Ethiopia sent to Slavery Offenses. On the boat of the Caribbean. In the biblical times. We can read, from our bible Scriptures. That the people of Kush, are the children of Israel who are refer to as the children of the Caribbean.

With this fact. Which has been presented time after time. By the Rastafarian community.

(Read the full verse) a verse of the recovery of the lost Tribes of Israel

And it shall come to pass
In the day that the Lord, shall set his hand again. The second time. To recover the remnant.
Of his people.
Which shall be left from Asyria and from Egypt
And from pathros and from Kush
And from Elan
And from Hamath, and from the islands
Of the sea. Isaiah 11:11

What is Rastafarianism

The Rastafarian community is a community of truth. By using word, songs, power. Knowledge of the bible and the teachings of his Majesty Emperor Haile Selassie the first.

Many people are being called into the crown of Thrones. Many of the Rastafarian community. Are representing this livity of the teachings and knowledge of his Majesty.

Let's start with the teachings of the beauty of the Lion of judah flag.

1. The color green on the flag
2. Represents. Green - for the beauty and vegetation of Ethiopia.
3. The gold stripe represents the wealth of Africa.
4. The red stripe represents the blood of the Martyrs.
5. The Lion represents: The Tribe of judah.

The flag of Judah
Is in full definition
Of our love for the Solomonic Dynasty of the world Ethiopia. And the love we share, for the Conquering lion of the Tribe of judah.

Bible study time

Are you not as children of the Ethiopians
Unto me. Children of Israel. Said the lord.
Have not I bought up Israel out of the land of Egypt? And The phillitians from caphtor and the Syrians from kir. . Amos 9:7

And it shall come to pass in that day.
That the Lord, shall set his hand again the second time to recover what belongs to his people. Which shall be left, from Assyria, and, from Egypt. And from psthros and from kush and from Elam . And from Shinar. And from Hamath and from the islands of the sea.. Isaiah 11:11

From this teaching of the scriptures
We know that the Solomonic Dynasty is the covenant of the Tribe of judah. We also now, know, and, understand it is written in the scriptures that The Ark of The Covenant, was given to Menelik the 1st. Gifted to him by his Father. King Solomon. We also know that the Ark of the Covenant. Lays in the holiness of the Angels. In the presence of the holy ghost.

We also know, and, recognize that the Ark of the covenant is where the lord, wants it to be. For we spiritually know, that man in flesh. Can't see the Ark of the covenant.
For only the eyes, of the Righteous and the congregation of the holy children. Could have, such access to the Ark of the covenant.
Especially in this time.

Upon the death of Queen Makeda Menelik the 1st. Assumed his Throne. And began ruling Around 950. B.C. The Ethiopian Solomonic Dynasty, continue to ruled. Until Emperor Haile Selassie the first, came to a end.
In 1974. So we no the Solomonic Dynasty did exist.

The Ark of the Covenant

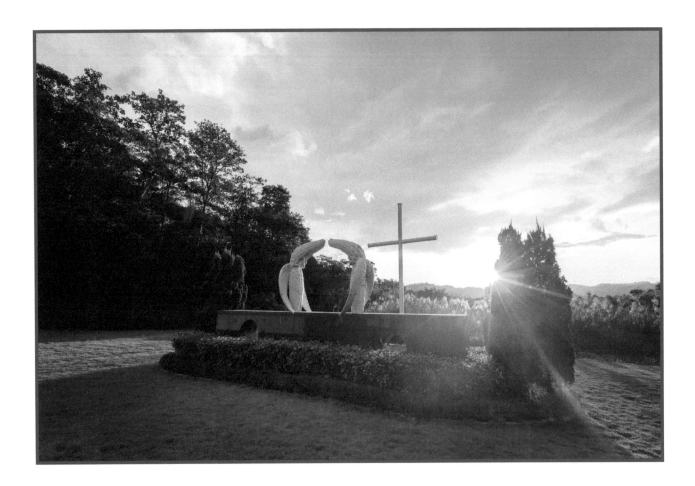

Through the years and centuries
Ethiopian people, have claim to have the Ark of The covenant. Hidden in a church. In the Small town of Aksum. In the northern highlands of Ethiopia. For many have, toured, studied, and, documented from the land of Ethiopia. Trying to find, answers to the questions of the Covenant. And still noone
Has come up, with a answer. To wear, the covenant dwells. Or if it ever existed.

Many will say it doesn't exist.
Because they can't find it.
Most people belief, is if you can't see it
Then it doesn't exist. But I do believe in the everlasting truth and power of the story, that exist in the Scriptures, and, in the stories

Given by, many priests, and, Anthropologists. It seems to be a everlasting blessing of judah. Given to the people of
Ethiopia. By Menelik The 1st. The first Emperor to ruled on The Ethiopian. Solomonic Dynasty. .

Being introduced to the love of Jesus Christ

I remember growing up in the city of Motown. Detroit Michigan. I was a little 6 year old. With many questions about the Almighty God.

My grandmother was a devoted catholic.

And I went to catholic school, in Detroit Michigan. And I attended Catholic church.
I recognize the anointing of the living God. Very early in life. I can remember asking my grandmother, can God see us, when we pray?

And I can remember her, saying yes he sees us, and hear us, when we are praising him and praying to him.....she would pray, many times, a day. In the sanctuary. I was so happy when, my grandmother told me, God could hear us. I started to pray even more. When praying for a barbie doll.

I learned very early, how the power of prayers can move many mountains.

I learned to love the Almighty God. And to Also fear the lord. I can remember many days, going to bible class, with my grandmother and family. I can remember wanting to better, understand the word of God.

And wanting to feel the power of the holy spirit. Even as a young child. I love to see the people on television. Recieving the holy spirit. And speaking in tongues. I would love to see the people, getting the holy ghost, and dancing in the isles of the church.

I wanted to feel that power. The power of the holy spirit. For to speak in his spirit. Is the best gift, anyone can imagine. I didn't feel that kind of power, when I was in the Catholic church. I wanted to understand why I didn't feel, or see, people in the sanctuary. Praising the lord. Like I had seen, in other churches.

I couldn't understand why. I was too young to understand, or, comprehend, the holy spirit. I just knew, what I felt inside my soul. I didn't understand the meaning of the holy spirit..until I got to be of the age of 16. I can remember, when I was 16. I seen my, bestfriend mom.
Receive the holy ghost. I can remember the minister, preaching, and the congregation shouting and dancing in spirit. Many were speaking tongues. I can remember seeing people falling out, and running, along the church. It was spiritually blessed, and, Amazing. The sound of the church Rhythmatic, musical beats. Mesmerize my Soul.

As I sat in church. I can remember thinking back, to when I was a child of 8 years old.
And my family and I, we're preparing, for the Baptism of my brothers and I. I can remember driving with my family, to church.
It was a hot summer Sunday morning. In the year of 85 . I can remember the preacher, preaching. It seemed like, he was preaching to me. I can remember, my family sitting in the front roll. Of the church. We were anticipating the baptism of my brothers and I.

I remember my oldest brother, went up first.
He felt the holy ghost fire. When he was place in the everlasting power of the holy water. He shouted to glory. Hallelujah.
The spirit of the lord, was in the church.
Everyone, was, shouting to glory.

Then the preacher, told my youngest brother
To come up, unto the alter. My little brother
Ran up to the Altar, shouting to Glory.

The preacher place, him in the Holy ghost water. My little brother, was shouting to glory. And the congregation of the church.
We're praising the lord. Hallelujah. It was so beautiful and blessed.

Then the preacher looked,at me and said.
Jammie Desiree, give me your hands.
I recognize the anointing of the lamb
Was in our church house. So admittedly, I grab, the hand, of our preacher. And I went up straight to the holiness of the water.

As the preacher started to pray over me
I close my eyes. I could see a vision of children of all races, nationalities. Starring at me, with big smiles. They were sitting around the lord. The children were wearing badge and white, color clothing. Dress all the same
We're the children. I opened my eyes, to see the preacher was still, hmmm praying for me.
I was feeling divine blessings.

He then place me, in the everlasting power of the holy ghost water.
I started to speak in tongues. I started to feel that holy ghost fire. I felt like I was floating around the Throne of king David. Solomon.
It was, beautiful. I felt like I was flying above the ceiling of the church. It was the first experience I received from the cross.
I was so excited to be save. Born again.
My parents were happy too.

Later on that day, at church service. We we're told, by the church mother. We all shall soon meet downstairs in the church dinning room for dinner, before church dismissal. All the children including myself, had to go downstairs to the church dinning room area.

As I started running towards, the stairs
I felt a comforting feeling divine blessings. I ran downstairs, vastly, fastly. As I was running full speed, down the stairs. I look up and there was, the Emperor Haile Selassie the first. Standing in the dinning room area.

He was standing very straight. He looked, right at me. I felt as if his eyes pierce my soul.
He was wearing a black, crush velvet suit. With a green lime sash, over his chest.
He wore many medals, he was very short in height. There he stood, like the king he was. I stood there. I didn't scream, I couldn't.
I didn't run, or, move. I couldn't.
I just stood there. In shock. I still had no clue who he was. But I knew by the feeling, he was a Spiritual leader.

I ran backup and scream for my mom.
My mom shouted at me. Child what is wrong with you? You look like you seen a ghost.

I scream mommy, there is a man, downstairs standing, in the living room. What man? My mom replied. I said mom that's the man. I seen downstairs in the basement. My mom
Replied, you mean the picture of the man
On the wall? Yes mommy, I replied. She began laughing. She said, that is His Majesty. Emperor Haile Selassie the first.
How could you had seen him? He is not alive, anymore.

I then stated but he's downstairs in the basement church, in the living room.
My mom grab my dad, and my dad, grab the minister. And the whole, congregation. Ran downstairs in the basement dinning room.
Everybody started praising the lord. And shouting, speaking in tongues.

The church congregation, started to pray over me.......hallelujah. I was then announce. I was then a child of the Almighty jah Rastafari. I then knew that, His Majesty Emperor Haile Selassie the first. Jah Rastafari.

I knew that the Emperor Haile Selassie the first. Was The Conquering lion of The Tribe of judah.

From this Spiritual experience. I have search
And research. Many rekindles of His Majesty Emperor Haile Selassie the first. JAH Rastafari.

To my personal experience with the spirit of truth. And perseverance. I have a clearer, understanding. Of the bible and the teachings of his Majesty. Emperor Haile Selassie the first. And yet . I still can't seem, to find a living Church, religious institution, that has, or can . Express oneself, in the religious philosophy of His Majesty. Emperor Haile Selassie the first. JAH Rastafari.

Life after death

The year was 2016, I was working part time at a Small hair salon. As a cosmetologist.
I was so happy, because I had a great weekend, I had a blessed work day. All my clients were style and looking gorgeous.
I had finish my last client. When my boss
Ask me, to drop off, our paperwork for the day, at the bank.

I remember this day, like it was yesterday.
I clean up, the beauty shop. And prepared
For my journey, to the bank.
That day, I took my same route. As usual .
I didn't realize or see the head on, collision that came my way. I remember driving singing. In my car. And suddenly boom .
Boom, bam. I was hit, head on.

I remember my car spinning out of control
Fastly, I felt like, the wind just knock me out
Of my body….I was suddenly. In my vehicle
Up, side down. And when I say, I was up side down. I mean it, literally speaking.

I remember the sky was, in my face.
After I was passing out, I remember my car was very hot…it was, burning due to the model of the vehicle. It was a 1994 fiero.
And I don't know, if you can remember.
The engine was built, in the back.
I recognize the sound of a lady, screaming
Drag her out, The car is on fire!!!

People were shouting for help.
I pass out ! . From that moment.
When I awaken, I was crying
Screaming, where am I ?. I scream please
Help me, I'm in pain. The doctor subdued me. With medication. I was so much confuse, I didn't know or, understand
What had happen. The doctor explained. I needed surgery on my neck, rightaway.

I agreed with that notion. I was prep. For emergency surgery. In my time of preparing for my surgery. I began to pray, to the Almighty JAHJAH. I remember saying . The lords, prayer, over, & over again. I felt a sense of contention and peace.

As I layed, laying down. Awaiting for my surgery to begin. My doctor, comes in the room, holding my chart. He said, to me
Hi ms. Jamie, how are you feeling? I responded. I'm worried and a little scared.
But I believe in the lord. He then looked at me
And said yes, we will do our best. To remove the tumor from your cervical. And we will be sure, to place a bracket in your neck.

I then replied !!!. Oh no what Tumor. The doctor, then replied. There is a tumor sitting on your neck, and it is bending your neck, & spinal cord. We must drain the flowing of fluid around it. And remove the tumor, entirely. So I responded, I am ready, prepared, I have the Almighty JAHJAH

By my side. The doctor then said.
There is a 50- 50 chance. You could die
Or even comeback paralyze. From this surgery. It is a risky surgery. Do you still, want to do it ?
He ask. Yes I responded. I'm in tremendous pain. As I was being put to sleep, by Anesthetic. I said take me jesus with you.

And jesus responded, he took me with him.
There I was, hovering in a cloud, next to a Angel of the lord. The Angel said, jammie
Look !!!. As I look up in the cloud. I seen jesus Christ. He was sitting on a beautiful translucent colored horse. Around the horses nk head was a Crown. The lord is beautiful. Hallelujah

I then seen the lord, lift up, his arm. Holding a sword, in his hand. Then I seen fire swords
Coming out, of the horses mouth. The lord was beautiful. He looked like The morning Star. So beautiful. He appeared to be of the age of 30 plus. He wore long twisted hair locks. Down to his back. He appeared to be
A man of color. He was wearing long clothes

He was wearing many beautiful garments
A white rob, and a beautiful dark colored rob
Like a burgundy color, but the color appeared to be, a undescribe color . Like a color, I never seen before. He was shinning
And sparks of glitter and small baby Angels
We're all around him. Trumpets I heard, all around us. I then seen, a door open up
The doors slided, glided openly. As if I was in a movie. When the doors slided openly.

I could hear, and, see the Army of the lord
They were wearing soldier clothing, riding upon horses. I could hear, the galloping of the horses. The lord then spoke to me. And said

Jammie go and tell the people. What you seen here. Tell them to get ready. Because I am coming soon. Then suddenly I saw African women, dancing around him.

The African women, were throwing roses
Around the Throne. The Thrones, were
Many. So tall I couldn't see the ending of the Thrones. There was fire all Around the Thrones. But it was beautiful in color. I didn't feel any heat…. I saw many in his Army. The Army was, so long. I couldn't see the ending of his Army. I then heard the lord, cry out.
Oh my people !!!. He then appeared in the sky. He was crying. Hallelujah. SELAH.

He was crying for Us. I then seen with the Angel next to me. A long table. And at that time, I seen Kwame nukuma, Malcom x.
And then Emperor Haile Selassie the first.
They were sitting at a long table, together. In peace tranquility and love. I ask the Angel
What is the table. She replied. It is the Holy table. Only his special Angels sit there.
The table was so long. There was no ending. I tried to see the ending table. But I couldn't see the ending. There was no ending.
Glory hallelujah.

Upon my awakening after surgery. I couldn't explain myself to my doctors.
I tried to talk, but I couldn't speak. Due to the surgery. But I wrote my testimony for my doctor to read. After he read my testimony.
He explained to me, that many of his patients, who had surgery, had Express experience with the spirit of God. After anistesha during surgery treatment. I told him, no this was real. I was there !!! . I really went there.
I started to explain, my experience with the lord. JAH Rastafari

My doctor started, too believe me. He responded by saying. Yes I too, had a similar experience. I was so happy to hear that from him. I thought that. I was going crazy.
But I knew that, what God allowed me to see
Was a Revelation blessing. From that experience. I learned to appreciate life
More then ever, before. For we never know
When our time is near.

From this perspective of life after death
I now no Longer, worry about day to day
Living life. For I seen the afterlife.
And heaven is beautiful.

But heaven send me back. Hallelujah
So I know I still got work to do. Work.of writing books, with Spiritual intervention
- And uplifting vibrations. Work to testify to the youth, and teach them. The love of jesus Christ.. And the love and. Teachings of His Majesty..Emperor Haile Selassie the first. JAHJAH Rastafari.

The Unveiling of the A.c.f.m Ministry
(Meeting Denroy Morgan)

(Bible study time)

(psalm 34) verse 15.

The eyes of the lord are upon
The Righteous. And his ears
Are open unto their cry.

(Revelation ch 5. Verse1.)

And I saw in the right hand
 Of him . That sat on the
  Throne. A book written
  Within and on the
   Backside " seal with 7
   Seals.

   (Revelation) ch5. Verse 5.

And one of the elders saith unto me weep not. Behold. " The lion of the Tribe of judah. The Root of David hath prevailed. To open the book of life. And to loose the 7 seals.

The year was 2017 . I had just recovered from my car accident. And I was living life
In blessings and love. I was appreciating life
More then ever before. After my accident
Surgery, the message I recieve & the
Annointing I felt, after seeing the afterlife
And the congregation of the Messiah yeshua.

I was ready to conquer the world.
I had recieve a second chance
And I was so thankful, grateful
Hallelujah. But I was still searching.
Searching for Spiritual intervention.
Searching for Spiritual freedom
Searching for Spiritual annoutment.
Searching for Spiritual guidance.

For after receiving a Spiritual blessing
I wanted to share it, I wanted to speak on it
I wanted to pass it on…. hallelujah(holy ghost).. fire.   Glory hallelujah.

So there I was still searching for Spiritual
Intervention.   And there it was. Right in front of me…..The blessings of judah. The Spirit of
the Redeemer through word & power, and , sound. Hallelujah. (heart of fire) . There it was
loud & clear. On my computer screen.
There was the ministry, I had been searching for.   The A.c.f.m Ministry.

I was breathtaking by the words, of This sanctified holy ghost fire voice. And it was
Coming from a Elder man. Who I had never
Heard of before. But I wanted to find out
More about this fire… the fire of the blessings of judah and the congregations of his Majesty.
His Imperial Majesty Emperor Haile Selassie the first. Rastafari. Holy jah. Rastafari.

So there I was stuck on my computer screen.
Watching this minister, preaching to the people of the Society of Social.
I was looking to watch him again. And so I did.   Every Sabbath Saturday morning.
I was tuned in. Learning, studying and recognizing the importance of the A.c.f.m ministry. I
began to recognize the anointing of the A.c.f.m ministry creed.

I started to recognize the anointing of denroy Morgan. Hallelujah glory to jah Rastafari.
I began to become unveiled. I began to become spiritually conscious, and, aware
That all that I was looking for. Was right in front of me all alone. My Spiritual veil was remotely,
remove.

I began to follow Mr. Morgan and his ministry.
For 3 years and to come.   For years, I searched, I looked, and never could I find
His Majesty Emperor Haile Selassie the first.
Teachings to be recognized, by a ministry
That not only recognizes the annointing of the holy spirit. But also recieve and recognize
The blessings of Judah and the Covenant of King David. King Solomon. But understand and
recognizes the importance of the 12 tribes of Israel.

But The A.c.f.m ministry recognizes
That his Majesty Emperor Haile Selassie the first. Is the Restoring Messiah.
And the Conquering lion of the Tribe of judah.
For as a family ministry.   They recognize the anointing of family and the love of the Messiah.
Yeshua. The Alpha and Omega

       (bible study time)

    (the Beatitudes)
Blessed are the poor in Spirit
For there's is the kingdom of heaven.

Blessed are the meek
For they shall inherit the earth.

Blessed are the peacemakers
For they shall be called
The children of God.

Blessed are the pure in heart
For they shall see God.

Blessed are they which do hunger
And thirst after Righteousness
For they shall be filled

Blessed are they that mourn
For they shall be comforted.

Blessed are the merciful
For they shall obtain mercy.

(The Conquering lion shall break every chain).

(Genesis to Revelation)

The lion of judah shall break every chain.

(bible study time)

It is vain for you to rise up early
To sit up late. To eat the bread of sorrows.
(psalm 127:2).

(Bible study time)

In The beginning Jah created the heavens and the earth.
(Genesis 1. Ch1)

Author closure

Over the years of my life. I have studied, read, research many writings about Emperor Haile Selassie the first. But never have I seen anyone, write of His Majesty Emperor Haile Selassie the first. In the heavens.

Many tell stories about His Majesty.

Many rekindles and love. Historical events and speeches, including the famous league of Nations, Speech. Which has, become phenomenal in every expression . He has Spoken. I pray His Majesty Emperor Haile Selassie the first. Never be forgotten in The world of books and Social media and Religious communities. Rastafari .

Author closure

I pray this short story. Has been presented with blessings and Honour and love.
I pray my short story, has been a blessed testimony &, Revelation that has, awaken
Others too the love of jesus Christ. And the blessings of judah. And the manifestation
Masonically through the teachings of His Majesty. Emperor Haile Selassie the first.
JAH Rastafari. Konjo meaning beautiful in the Amharic Ethiopian language.

Hallelujah glory to the king. My lord and savior.
Glory & blessings to His Majesty.
Emperor Haile Selassie the first.
JAH Rastafari.

Written by: lady Jammie Desiree.
A darling daughter of His Majesty.
Written on: 01/ 10/ 20.